Women With ADHD

The Ultimate ADHD In Women Guide To Stay Organised, Improve Relationships, And Manage Your Emotions. Learn To Live A Better Life With Proven & Highly Effective Strategies.

Giselle Branson

Legal Notice:
Copyright 2022 by Giselle Branson - All rights reserved.

This document is geared towards providing exact and reliable information regarding the topic and issue covered. The publication is sold on the idea that the publisher is not required to render an accounting, officially permitted, or otherwise, qualified services. If advice is necessary, legal or professional, a practiced individual in the profession should be ordered.
From a Declaration of Principles which was accepted and approved equally by a Committee of the American Bar Association and a Committee of Publishers and Associations.

Legal Notes:
In no way is it legal to reproduce, duplicate, or transmit any part of this document by either electronic means or in printed format. Recording of this publication is strictly prohibited and any storage of this document is not allowed unless with written permission from the publisher. All rights reserved.

The information provided herein is stated to be truthful and consistent, in that any liability, in terms of inattention or otherwise, by any usage or abuse of any policies, processes, or directions contained within is the solitary and utter responsibility of the recipient reader. Under no circumstances will any legal responsibility or blame be held against the publisher for any reparation, damages, or monetary loss due to the information herein, either directly or indirectly. Respective authors own all copyrights not held by the publisher.

Disclaimer Notice:
The information herein is offered for informational purposes solely and is universal as so. The presentation of the information is without a contract or any type of guarantee assurance. Readers acknowledge that the author is not engaging in the rendering of legal, financial, medical or professional advice. Please consult a licensed professional before attempting any techniques outlined in this book.
The trademarks that are used are without any consent, and the publication of the trademark is without permission or backing by the trademark owner. All trademarks and brands within this book are for clarifying purposes only and are the owned by the owners themselves, not affiliated with this document.

Table of Contents

Fundamentals Of ADHD – Everything You Need To Know 4

Symptoms Of ADHD You Might Be Unaware Of 9

How Does ADHD Differ In Women And Men And What To Do About It? 15

Executive Function And The Hyperactive Mind 20

5 Powerful Executive Function Strategies 27

How To Quickly Improve Your Focus With Proven Strategies 34

Simple Step By Step Strategies To Declutter Your Life 38

Isolation And Social Dysfunction 43

How To Meet New People, Form New Friendships, and Pursue Romantic Relationships 46

How To Improve Your Current Relationships With Proven Tactics 49

Best Jobs For Women With ADHD 54

Improve Your Spending Habits In An Easy And Sustainable Way 60

Fall Asleep Faster And Sleep Better On A Regular Basis 64

Fundamentals Of ADHD – Everything You Need To Know

If you have had a recent diagnosis of ADHD, or even if you have had a diagnosis for a long time, you might want to know more about what ADHD involves and how it impacts your life. So, what are the fundamental factors of ADHD?

ADHD does not mean the same thing for every individual, which is one of the things that can make this very difficult to understand. Even if you know other people with ADHD, you may find that you struggle to pinpoint which symptoms actually relate to your ADHD, and which are simply aspects of your personality. Figuring this out can be enormously helpful, however, because it will give you a much better understanding of yourself and your behaviour.

Recognising that ADHD presents differently in different people is a fundamental part of understanding this condition, especially if you know other people with ADHD, or you read a lot about the topic. Remember that you do not need to tick every box and fit every description. Simply take what is useful to you, and discard information that feels irrelevant or doesn't speak to you.

With that said, let's start understanding the fundamental aspects of ADHD.

One of the first things to mention is that ADHD is often less pronounced in women, and many women are better able to mask their symptoms. This doesn't mean that the symptoms don't exist, but you should start by being aware that you may hide certain aspects of your condition better than other people do. Remembering this may help you to better assess which symptoms do and don't speak to you.

Now, let's look at how ADHD commonly presents itself. There are 3 kinds of ADHD, which are characterised by their symptoms. One type is known as primarily inattentive, and its main symptoms are distraction and disorganisation.

The second type is known as hyperactive or impulsive ADHD, and unsurprisingly, its main symptoms are hyperactivity and impulsiveness. The third type is a combination of both, and it is known as combined ADHD. These are not hard and fast categories, and they can change to some extent as the person grows and their environment changes.

A lot of women find that they have difficulty getting a diagnosis of ADHD, perhaps because they tend to be better at masking the symptoms. It is worth noting that at present, experts don't believe you can develop ADHD in adulthood; it must be present from childhood. Often, the symptoms are more easily seen among children, so let's look at these first.

The symptoms of inattentive ADHD tend to include:

- Being easily distracted
- Having a short attention span
- Constantly wanting to switch from one task to another
- Struggling to organise tasks
- Having trouble with tasks that are time-consuming or tedious
- Struggling to follow instructions
- Misplacing things
- Forgetting things
- Making mistakes due to carelessness

The symptoms of hyperactive ADHD include:

- Little sense of danger
- Being incapable of sitting still
- Struggling to focus on a task
- Constantly moving
- Talking excessively
- Struggling with turn-taking
- Doing things without thinking about the consequences
- Interrupting people when they are talking

Combined ADHD, unsurprisingly, will have aspects of both of these conditions. It may be more one than the other, but it is still seen as combined.

Those are the major characteristics of ADHD in children. They are often more evident in children, because many adults find ways to cope with the symptoms and become better at masking them. However, if you recognise these as things that you have struggled with in the past, there's a chance that you still struggle with them and you have simply improved your strategies.

That said, medical professionals have found it much harder to define the symptoms for adults, and a lot of them do change. It is thought that the condition has quite different effects on adults, and hyperactivity often decreases. Unfortunately, with the intense pressure that often accompanies adulthood, inattentiveness can become a considerably more difficult problem.

You might recognise some or all of the following:

- Poor organisation skills
- Difficulty with prioritising
- Difficulty with focusing
- Constantly moving to new tasks, and not completing old tasks

- Being forgetful
- Difficulty with keeping quiet and constantly talking over other people
- Speaking without stopping to think
- Unpredictable moods and sudden mood swings
- Difficulty with coping when stressed
- Impatience
- Lack of attention to detail
- Misplacing things regularly
- Partaking in risky activities
- Edginess and difficulty with relaxing

Obviously, some of those do overlap with the symptoms of ADHD in children, which isn't surprising. However, if you have had ADHD since childhood, it is worth thinking about the ways in which your condition has changed and what new symptoms may have developed as you have aged.

Symptoms Of ADHD You Might Be Unaware Of

You are probably already aware of many of the symptoms mentioned in the previous chapter, which are commonly associated with ADHD. However, this condition can be surprisingly varied, and there are symptoms that many people don't know about, or forget about. Recognising these more unusual aspects of the condition will improve your understanding of it, so let's look at some of these.

Impulse Buying

Have you ever found that you buy things without really thinking about it? Have you ever gone into a shop intending to just look around, and come out with your arms full of bags and boxes of things that you're not sure you really wanted or needed?

You might start to worry about whether you are materialistic or you just have bad impulse control – but this could actually be your ADHD taking over and making your life harder. ADHD makes it harder to think about the consequences of doing something, which may make it considerably more difficult to stick to a budget, or to think about what will happen if you spend money that you might need later.

Other symptoms, like lack of attention to detail, inability to focus, and difficulty with prioritising may also play into impulse buying habits and make it difficult to ignore things when you want them.

Boredom Intolerance

A lot of people find it difficult to deal with being bored, but people with ADHD are far less likely to cope well with boredom. It exacerbates many of the symptoms, including difficulty focusing and difficulty sitting still. Boredom can also trigger anxiety, rather than just a sense of frustration or lethargy.

This presents a real challenge for many working women with ADHD; if you have to undertake tasks that you find unengaging, you will have particular difficulty in toughing it out and slogging your way through the task. That means you need to think about what work is appropriate for you, what the potential drawbacks of your chosen career may be (e.g. does it frequently involve tasks that you will find unengaging and frustrating?), and how you can overcome these.

In some cases, you may be able to work with an employer to assign certain tasks that you find difficult to other people. Sometimes, you will have to find other workaround strategies. Recognising the difficulties that you face in terms of boredom intolerance will make it easier for you to play to your strengths and avoid your weaknesses.

Hyper Focusing

Although many people view ADHD as a condition that makes it hard to focus, one of the less-recognised symptoms is hyper focusing. This makes it difficult for people with ADHD to switch from one task to another, and encourages them to focus heavily on one thing instead. While this can have benefits, it can also be an issue, because it makes it difficult to cope with a distracting environment. You may find that you take longer to respond to distractions, and longer to get back to your original activity afterwards.

Again, recognising this challenge as one that you face is often a great way to ensure you avoid environments that exacerbate the issue, and choose ones that will help to make the most of your tendency to hyperfocus.

Emotional Sensitivity

This one is very rarely associated with ADHD, but it is a surprisingly common symptom. A lot of people think that those with ADHD don't deal with emotions well, and this can lead to the mistaken belief that they don't feel emotions – when it actually tends to be the opposite. People with ADHD often struggle to deal with emotions, but they can still feel them, and sometimes very intensely.

If you find that you respond to criticism or rejection in negative ways and become defensive or hostile, it may be because your ADHD is taking control of how you feel. You need to be aware of the impact that this condition can have on your emotions, and how difficult it can be to control them. Try to actively work on accepting criticism when it is useful to you, and not making a blanket rejection of all criticism.

Sleep Issues

Do you have trouble falling asleep? If so, there is a chance that this is linked with your ADHD – because a vast majority of people who suffer from ADHD also suffer from sleep difficulties. This unfortunately often leads to fatigue, which can make symptoms like forgetfulness and lack of focus much worse than they would otherwise be.

Sleep problems can be difficult to tackle and immensely frustrating to deal with, because they are often long-term and they can garner surprisingly little sympathy from people who do not suffer from them. If you find that you struggle to doze off or that your sleep is broken and you frequently wake up throughout the night, it may be much harder to function. You should talk to your doctor about this, and be aware that your ADHD is probably a contributing factor.

Emotional Outbursts

If you find that your emotions get the better of you at unexpected times and you feel like you're always operating on a short fuse, this might be a result of ADHD. Many people who suffer from this condition struggle to regulate their emotions and keep them in check. You might find that you feel angrier than a situation warrants, or that you struggle to deal with feelings of unhappiness.

This can make it difficult to establish strong, caring relationships with others. If other people get frustrated with you and feel that you need to better get a grip on your emotions, remember that this could be due to your ADHD.

While you will still need to learn tactics to better manage your feelings, you should be kind to yourself and make a point of recognising that it isn't your fault and you aren't being unreasonable.

Those are some of the more unusual symptoms that are caused by ADHD, which you may not be aware of. There are of course many other symptoms that ADHD can either cause directly or contribute to, so it's always worth doing some research if there is a symptom that you are concerned about and you want to know if it relates to ADHD.

How Does ADHD Differ In Women And Men And What To Do About It?

Given that so much of the information relating to ADHD is written in regards to men, you might be wondering how this differs for women, and what you might need to know about how ADHD affects you specifically. There are a few ways in which ADHD is thought to have particular effects on females, so let's explore these. Women everywhere deserve to understand this.

So far, it is thought that men and women both experience much the same symptoms and to the same degree. It is thought that medication has a similar effect on both men and women, that the struggles faced are comparable, and that they are equally likely to suffer from other related disorders as a result of the condition. That might make it sound like ADHD doesn't have a different impact on women – but several studies have proven otherwise. It is thought that even if ADHD appears in the same manner across the sexes, women may suffer considerably more from the effects than men do. You might be wondering why, and there's no simple answer – but the truth is that women are often grappling with things like hormone fluctuations, reduced self-belief, an increased risk of self-harm, and the problems associated with gender roles.

It is thought that the combination of these things means that ADHD could mean that women who suffer from this condition are massively disadvantaged.

For example, a woman who struggles to control her emotions at work as a result of ADHD is much more likely to be labelled "bitchy," "emotional," "unstable," or "unreliable." A man might face repercussions, but these are not likely to be to the same degree. Women tend to have to work harder to be seen as rational and logical, and this involves more regulation of emotions.

Similarly, women are often expected to be better at soft skills like time management and organisation. Many people dismiss it when a man struggles with these things, because they see men as less capable, but they expect women to cope to a greater degree.

It is also thought that women tend to understate how they are feeling, and minimise their struggles. Because many women work in the home, being overwhelmed by something may be seen as less valid than a man in a workplace. Tasks such as laundry and childcare are often viewed as less stressful, even though they can be as valid and challenging as workplace tasks – and unfortunately, this leads to many women with ADHD being dismissed as overly emotional, both by others and by themselves.

They may doubt their capabilities, and distrust their own sense of being overwhelmed and needing a break.

Additionally, many women fall into the role of being the caregiver and the support network for those around them, which puts additional pressure on them not to break down and lean on others. They also take on the bulk of household tasks and responsibilities, and may be working alongside that, pushing themselves to do more than men and requiring more of themselves.

There's also a risk that women will feel guiltier for uncontrolled outbursts, as these tend to be directed at children or partners, which can have a greater emotional toll. If you don't recognise that these outbursts are triggered by your ADHD, you are likely to spiral into self-blame.

In terms of hormones, both progesterone and oestrogen interact with ADHD and may in some ways make ADHD easier to deal with – but when the premenstrual hormone levels decrease, the symptoms of ADHD tend to get worse. Lack of oestrogen can result in more irritation, and more problems with concentrating. It can also cause reduced ability to sleep and mood slumps.

ADHD can also become more challenging to deal with once the oestrogen levels drop following menopause.

A lot of women find that their ADHD can get harder to deal with once menopause is over, although a lot more research is needed to understand this.

That might leave you wondering what to do about it. Unfortunately, there are no easy answers, but hopefully recognising how ADHD might affect you in different ways may make your life easier. If nothing else, it should help to alleviate feelings of guilt, and might encourage you to seek more support and help from your partner, your friends, or other people in your life.

You should also take this as a sign to be kinder to yourself, and not to push harder than is fair. Be understanding of your own difficulties with time-keeping and don't take on tasks that are specifically contrary to your skills. A major part of excelling in life involves recognising where your strengths lie and playing to them as much as you can.

It is also worth investing time in building the skills that you struggle with. For example, if you know that you find time-keeping a challenging thing, you should spend some time developing strategies that will help you. Diaries, planners, calendars, and apps may all encourage you to stay on track and make life easier for you. Try different strategies until you find the ones that work for you, and then keep using these to make life easier wherever possible.

The combination of these two approaches – recognising and accepting the things you find hard, and trying to find tricks that will make them at least a little easier – should improve your general well-being and make you feel better.

Executive Function And The Hyperactive Mind

You are probably already familiar with the term 'executive function,' but you may not have a full understanding of what this is and how it works. The term refers to the operation of the brain, and all the complex things that it does when functioning normally. It often refers to tasks like organising, managing, and categorising items. It can also refer to emotional processes or cognitive processes.

This then leads us to a second term: 'executive dysfunction.'

Executive dysfunction is defined as a range of difficulties that occur within the brain, usually as a result of a disorder. They may be behavioural, cognitive, or emotional, and they happen whenever the brain isn't functioning the way that it should, or is struggling with a task that a neurotypical brain would not generally struggle with much.

Many people who suffer from executive dysfunction cannot deal well with time management, problem-solving, or planning. They may also find organisation very challenging. Staying on task and keeping track of personal items can be very difficult. Executive dysfunction is often associated with the lack of ability to regulate emotions, too.

Essentially, your brain is functioning in a 'hyper' way that prevents you from focusing on these things in the way that a neurotypical person might. You cannot be diagnosed with executive dysfunction because this can be caused by many different conditions, and even certain injuries. It isn't always associated with ADHD, but many people with ADHD – if not all – will suffer from executive dysfunction.

Executive dysfunction can affect many different areas of your life, so we'll explore some of these in more detail below. You will notice that there is a lot of overlap with the difficulties we have already mentioned, because ADHD and executive dysfunction do heavily overlap with each other.

Attention And Concentration

Many people recognise that ADHD is almost always paired with attention problems, and indeed this is the first letter in the acronym. If you find that you easily get distracted and it's very challenging to stay on task, no matter what the task is, this is an aspect of executive dysfunction and the hyperactive mind. Your brain wants to do too many things at once, so it leaps from one to another without warning, and without you being able to control it.

Multitasking

Because of the problems with maintaining concentration, multitasking can be a nightmare for people with ADHD. Women in particular often end up trying to multitask, caring for children, cleaning the house, balancing finances, and working, along with trying to keep up a social life – and this can feel impossible. It is challenging enough for people with ADHD, but the multitasking aspect of executive functioning is excessively hard for those with ADHD.

Problem-Solving

Do you find that you struggle to come up with solutions to problems because you get bogged down in all the 'what if' and 'but then' scenarios? A lot of people who suffer from ADHD can find themselves going in circles when trying to solve a problem, because their initial solution doesn't seem right, so they go back to the problem, only to come up with the same solution again and again.

You might find that you feel paralysed by the potential negative outcomes, so you dwell more and more on the problem itself, rather than on overcoming it. This aspect of ADHD is often less recognised than others, but it can be debilitating.

Naming it and recognising when you are doing it may help you to get more focused on solutions, but you should also recognise that this is something you struggle with.

Emotional Control

If you find it hard to regulate how you feel, you should be aware that this is also a sign of executive dysfunction. Your brain is responsible, to an extent, for controlling your emotions, and if you can't stay in control, it's because your brain is grappling with emotions that are too big for it.

This again comes back to your brain trying to do too much at once, the hyperactive side of it. It struggles to focus on controlling your emotions because it isn't focused on that – and this leads to other problems too, like behavioural control.

If you can't control your emotions, it is far, far harder to control your behaviour. You may find that you act rashly and then regret it later, especially when you have acted in anger. You might rush into things without carefully thinking them through, or you might miss obvious solutions (due to a lack of problem-solving abilities) and take a less desirable course of action.

A lot of people with ADHD find that they are quick to anger – but they may also be quick to other emotions too.

If you often find yourself responding based on how you feel, you aren't alone and this is an aspect of how your brain functions. Learning how to slow down and take a more measured response may work, but it is often a technique that takes quite a lot of practice.

Memory

If you have to write a lot of things down, it is probably because of the way your brain processes information when you take it in the first time. Many people with ADHD find themselves frustrated by their memory issues, and they can be surprisingly large. If you find that you can't remember some fairly large event that everyone else swears you attended, this may be because your brain isn't set up to record memories the way that other people do.

Of course, that isn't to say that you will forget everything, but you should be aware that your retention is different from that of many neurotypical people, and it isn't your fault if you struggle to remember things. Again, you may find that you have to depend heavily on calendars and reminder systems, otherwise you may walk out of the door without the things you need – or even forget to walk out of the door when you need to.

Executive dysfunction can be associated with either minor memory issues or pretty severe ones. If you are struggling with your memory, it's worth talking to a doctor, but be aware that your brain likely struggles to retain information the way that others may do.

Time Management

Another common weakness of people with ADHD, poor time management is heavily associated with executive dysfunction and the hyperactive mind. Your brain is busy doing things other than watching the clock, and it isn't good at assessing how long it will take you to do certain tasks. You might think you only need to grab your jacket and put your shoes on before you leave, but if you have forgotten that you also need to find your keys and make some lunch, you're going to find yourself late a lot of the time. If you can't guess or you consistently underestimate how long tasks will take, it will make everything worse.

Time management is often an ongoing struggle for people who suffer from ADHD and executive dysfunction. You may find that your brain just isn't good at assessing tasks, measuring how long they will take, and prioritising them correctly so that they get done when they need to.

Time management draws on a lot of skills that people with ADHD struggle with, and this can make it one of the hardest things to do successfully. If you are already having difficulty remembering things, organising the materials you need, and working out what to prioritise, managing your time becomes almost impossible.

Fortunately, many of these things are areas that you can work on once you have identified them as things that you struggle with. There are a lot of techniques, tricks, and tools out there that will help you to improve things like your time management, and help you to remember. Sometimes, just acknowledging the things you find hard will make them less stressful and help you to navigate them more effectively.

Remember, your brain may be very active and this might make certain activities hard, but you can work with what you have as long as you understand it and you find strategies that help. That's what we'll cover in the next chapter.

5 Powerful Executive Function Strategies

In order to improve your executive function, you might find it helps to start employing certain strategies. In this section, we'll cover a few of the top ways that people can improve their executive function. Remember that these may not have an immediate impact, and not everybody will find them effective – but they may help you at least a little when it comes to managing the problems we have just discussed.

Strategy 1) Create A To-Do List That Works For You

You might feel like to-do lists are destined to fail, especially if you have tried to use them before and struggled – but don't give up. It can take time to figure out what sort of to-do list would work best for you, and to get into the habit of using it. Don't assume because it fails once, it can never be effective, and don't decide to stop using your list before you've given it a chance. That said, do look for one that genuinely helps you, and spend some time trialling different systems so you don't waste hours building to-do lists that go unheeded day after day.

Firstly, decide whether you think your to-do list should be digital or physical. Different people have different preferences. There are lots of apps that will help you to create to-do lists, but you may find that the act of writing the items down helps you to think about them.

A lot of people with ADHD find that having basic tasks on the list – as well as the more unusual ones like appointments – can help them to stay on track. For example, if you need to clean your house on Wednesdays, have this on your list, even if it's a weekly chore. It will remind you that it exists and make sure you leave time for it, rather than filling up your list with other things.

Some people find that it helps not to assign tasks to specific days (within reason; appointments and deadlines need specific days). Instead, making a general list of tasks that need doing might feel more comfortable for you. Use this to guide your daily actions, but don't put a specific task on one day rather than another. In some cases, this will help, while in others, it will lead to procrastination.

List-making needs to be done in a way that suits you, so take some time to get this right and figure out what you need from your list. If you need hard deadlines, implement these, and use a rewards system to encourage yourself to meet them.

If you work better with guidance but flexibility, create a general list and use it to fill in your days according to how you feel at the time.

This should make it much easier to turn to-do lists into a tool that helps you. If you just try to force a standardised system on yourself, they will probably become a major source of stress that you can't deal with, and you will stop using them.

Once you've established a system that works, put it somewhere prominent (so you see it) and be proud of yourself for using it. If you have a few off days or weeks, don't feel angry with yourself. Remember, this sort of organisation and time management is particularly difficult for you, and any attempt at it should be counted as a win.

Strategy 2) Build In More Time

This is a strategy that it may take a while to get the hang of, but it is well worth attempting it, especially if you find you are consistently late for things. Start building in an extra 10 to 15 minutes (or more if that makes sense for the given situation) so you can be sure you will arrive somewhere on time. Having the discipline to do this isn't always easy, but keep working at it, and you will find that you improve gradually.

You should work on completely convincing yourself that the earlier, false deadline is the true deadline. If you need to be at work for 9, start telling yourself 8:45, and genuinely think 8:45 any time you think about it. Correct yourself if you think "8:45, but really it's 9."

Imposing false deadlines can be done by entering things into your calendar 15 minutes earlier than they actually are. Keep doing this consistently, and you should find that you have more time. If you need to catch a train at 10:00, tell yourself that it is at 9:45, and aim to be at the station for 9:45. Lots of positive reinforcement may make this easier.

Some people also find that changing their clocks helps. If you set your clock to be 10 minutes fast, it can help encourage you to get moving. This doesn't work for everyone, but some people find it useful.

Strategy 3) Organise In Advance

This can be used in conjunction with the above strategy to ensure you are stepping out of the door at the right moment. If you normally have a flurry of activity and panic as you are leaving, try to offset this by doing the pre-leaving activities much sooner.

Create a checklist of the things you generally need before leaving, and have all of these things ready half an hour before you need to step out.

You may find it helps to put your bag by the door with things like your wallet, keys, notebook, phone, and anything else that you carry on a daily basis ready. Fill this bag around half an hour before you need to leave, and then have a quick out-the-door list that reminds you of anything you might need to do first (e.g. set alarm, close windows, lock up). This will mean that even if you are cutting it to the wire, the things you need are waiting by the door, so you are less likely to forget something important, like a work presentation, and you can step out quickly.

The out-the-door list can also help to mitigate any sense of concern after you've left the house, and may stop you from having to go back to do these tasks. All of these things should make it easier.

Parents in particular may benefit from advance planning, as getting small children out of the house to school and yourself off to work can be really difficult. In these cases, you might want to do the preparation the night before. Bags, homework, coats, and anything else your child needs should be waiting by the door before you go to bed that night.

This will save morning rushes, panics, and forgotten things, and makes it far, far more likely that you will be able to leave at a sensible time. It will also massively reduce your stress and make the mornings pleasanter for everybody, giving you more time to focus on things like breakfast, which cannot be done in advance.

Strategy 4) Ask For Help

A lot of people don't like asking others to help them when they are struggling, but doing so can be a wonderful mechanism for ensuring that you have the tools you need to do your job or to excel in your everyday life. Pinpoint some of the things that you find really hard and see if you can delegate them, whether at work or at home. If you find that you struggle with things like bill payments, regular chores, or keeping track of paperwork, see whether your partner would be willing to take on these tasks, while you tackle ones that play to your strengths. Some adults feel like this is cheating, but it isn't; it allows everybody to do the things that they are good at, and work efficiently. It can be harder if there is a task that both you and your partner/friend/family member/colleagues hate, but don't be afraid to ask and see whether they would be willing to lighten your load in exchange for some help in return.

Strategy 5) Review At The End Of The Day

When you have finished for the day, you might be tempted to just crash out with a movie or a good book, but try not to do this without taking a few minutes to review the day first. Think about the things that you achieved and the things that went well, and then think about what you would like to achieve tomorrow.

Keep a notepad by your bed so you can quickly and easily jot down notes when you think of things that you still need to do, or if there is something that you feel particularly proud of. Your daily review only needs to take a few minutes, but doing this will make you feel more in control of your life and should help you to identify if you're dropping balls somewhere at times.

Hopefully, implementing those 5 strategies will help you to feel more on track and encourage you to tackle some of the things that you find particularly difficult from day to day. If they don't work for you, don't despair; use other similar techniques or adapt them so that they will suit your needs.

How To Quickly Improve Your Focus With Proven Strategies

Focus is one of the hardest things for most individuals with ADHD, so you may find it particularly beneficial to look for strategies that will help with this. Not being able to focus can make any task feel virtually impossible, which means you should always be looking for ways to improve your focus. That is what we will cover in this section.

Strategy 1) Create A Good Environment

Take a few minutes to look at where you choose to work and what sort of environment it is. Are you operating in a busy space with people walking past, the TV on, music playing, the phone ringing, or kids playing outside? Remember, one of the things that people with ADHD particularly struggle with is swapping from one task to another, so if you are constantly distracted by the things around you, you're setting yourself up to fail. Instead, you should make your environment quiet and free from distractions. Remove comic books, games, and other items that are likely to take your attention away from the work you are doing, and focus on creating a work-tailored space with everything you need handy.

If you don't have to go and look for a pen every time you want to do some work, you're more likely to get the work done.

Consider turning your phone off when you are working on something important, wearing earphones or headphones to drown out sound, and closing programs that you don't need running while you work.

Strategy 2) Stick With One Thing

You might find it hard to stay focused on just one thing – that's sort of the nature of ADHD – but that doesn't mean you should give up on this entirely. Don't consciously engage in multiple tasks at once. Recognise that even though it's tempting, you are less likely to be productive and you will probably find that your tasks take a lot longer as a result. The quality may also go down considerably. Quite a lot of studies have been done on this, and it has been found that every time you switch task, you pay a "cost" as you re-focus and remember what you were doing. That cost makes multitasking inefficient even for many neurotypical people, but for people with ADHD, it can be massive. You should therefore set yourself up for success and aim to work on a single thing at once. Put other tasks away/out of sight until you have finished your current one so you don't pick them up and get distracted by mistake.

Strategy 3) Exercise

Many people who suffer from ADHD find that exercise is the answer to at least some of the difficulties they face. Remember that part of this disorder often involves hyperactivity, having excessive energy that you want to burn. If you don't start burning that energy, it is much harder for you to focus.

Not everybody with ADHD finds that exercise increases their ability to focus, but a lot do. Going for a long, tiring run can help your mind settle to things when you might otherwise struggle. Nobody knows exactly why exercise helps you to focus sometimes, but it clearly does for many people. Next time you feel your mind wandering or you have to keep dragging yourself back to your task, stop, do a bit of exercise for 10-20 minutes, and then return to it and see if your mind is clearer.

Strategy 4) Use Your Energy Peaks

A lot of people have ebbs and flows throughout the day as their productivity goes up and down. Figuring out when your "good" moments are and making use of these is critical. Are you at your best in the morning? Do you have a second wind after dinner? Do you lose all ability to focus when you've just had lunch?

Plan your days around this awareness and you will find your tasks are easier to get through. If you know you struggle to pay attention in the morning, assign easier tasks that require less brainpower to those moments, and tackle the harder stuff later on.

If you don't like having that much structure or you find your energy levels vary, this technique may not work. In this case, you should instead try to get in tune with how you are feeling at any given moment, and get into the habit of assessing what you are capable of doing at that point. Before sitting down to an activity, ask yourself how you are feeling, how focused you are, and whether you think it is the best current use of your energies.

These techniques should make it easier to focus, although it is important to recognise that for most people with ADHD, this is an ongoing battle that will never truly be won. Be proud of your efforts and utilise your time as efficiently as possible, and you should find that gradually, your level of focus increases. Often, training your focus is like training a muscle, so try to make it easy for yourself, keep practising, and you should improve.

Simple Step By Step Strategies To Declutter Your Life

Many people who have ADHD suffer because of clutter; it makes it so much harder to be organised if you live in a chaotic house with things on every surface. Unfortunately, this condition can also make it seriously hard to get rid of clutter. If you are feeling overwhelmed by the amount of stuff you have, you aren't alone.

Decluttering can make life a lot easier for everybody, but it's not easy to do when you are faced with something as overwhelming as a houseful of clutter. This applies tenfold if you have children. You might find some of the below strategies help you.

Strategy 1) Make A Plan

If you keep delaying, day after day, because you don't feel like you know where to start and the whole situation seems overwhelming, what you need is a plan.

You can start your plan by listing which rooms or areas of your home need decluttering. Prioritise the ones that you use most (e.g. your kitchen) so that you will feel the benefits of decluttering.

Next, schedule your decluttering efforts so that you actually make space in your calendar for them. Making a specific slot in which you will do, for example, 1 hour of decluttering can help to make the task less daunting, and makes you more likely to do it. Remember, slow and steady is often the best way to approach something like this. Don't try to declutter your whole home over the course of a weekend.

Some people find that it helps to have a specific day of the week in which they do some decluttering. Give this a try and see if you find it helps.

Strategy 2) Designate Boxes

If you have room for a few boxes in your home, create a "donate" box and a "sell" box for the things you sort. This can make it much easier to pick up something that you want to get rid of and simply put it in the correct box, so you can then address several things at once. Often, this works well if you have a lot of things that you wish to donate to a charity. It will help to make decluttering easier, because you'll have a designated spot to put the things you want to get rid of.

Strategy 3) Minimise Purchases

I mentioned earlier how hard it can be to avoid impulse buys when you suffer from ADHD – but you might find that you can limit how much you buy if you bear in mind that you will someday have to decide what to do with that item. Before buying anything, ask yourself how long you will need it for, what you will do with it when you no longer need it, and how much space it will take up in your home. You should find that this sort of process makes it easier to resist impulse buying.

It will short-circuit your "must have" instinct and help you to consider more rationally what joy that item will bring to you and how much energy you will have to invest in getting rid of it when the time comes.

Strategy 4) Avoid Handling Things

It might sound strange, but it has been shown that people are much more likely to want to keep things when they hold them. If you have just pulled out a forgotten blouse or old necklace, try not to sit and stare at it or hold it for longer than necessary. It may be easier to get rid of it if you make a quick decision to let it go.

Strategy 5) Label Things

Because so many people with ADHD struggle to organise, you might find it really difficult to put things away in appropriate places. Whenever you are decluttering, take some time to think about what categories you are dealing with, and write down your thoughts so that you can group objects in a way that makes sense to you. For example, if you are sorting out clothes, consider whether you could group summer shirts and winter shirts. Alternatively, tidy up paperwork by year or by usefulness. Group stationery by how frequently you need it.

Strategy 6) Put Things Away

This last strategy may sound too obvious to be useful, but sometimes, just increasing your awareness of how you handle objects is enough to make your life less cluttered. When you have used an item, try to be aware of what you do with it. Do you put it away, or do you simply put it down somewhere? If it's the latter, remember that you will then have to come back and put it away later – which has a time cost.

If you aren't sure where the item goes, that's a sign of something important: you need to find it a home. Where should that item live? Finding a place for these "drifting" items can help to cut down on clutter.

You may find that there is value in the phrase: only handle it once. Whenever you have an item in your hands, try to put it away and save yourself the time cost of having to pick it up again and put away later. Nobody is perfect at this and there will be times when you need to prioritise other things – but trying to make a habit of this can help.

Isolation And Social Dysfunction

It is thought that women with ADHD are particularly vulnerable to feelings of isolation. Men with ADHD can also find it difficult to connect with others, but it is commonly acknowledged that women are in a particularly difficult situation, and women are much more likely to notice the difficulties that they have and to feel them intensely.

Many women with ADHD face a double standard, because a lot of people feel that women ought to be good at socialising. Where men are often given a pass for poor social skills, women may end up disconnected and may struggle to feel connected to others. This can cause a sense of sadness and loneliness, and you might not even be sure why you struggle so much to connect with others – an enormously frustrating situation to find yourself in. Add these difficulties to the challenges presented by poor time management, lack of organisation, problems with switching from one task to another, and problems with emotional regulation, and it's no wonder that so many women who suffer from ADHD struggle when it comes to friendships. One of the ways in which you can start addressing this is to ask friends and family for feedback on how you could improve your social skills. Listen to their input and consider practising with somebody you trust.

Learning to regulate your emotions may also help, as this will make it easier for others to feel comfortable with you.

You can also make a point of verbalising what you need to feel more included. It is very hard sometimes to ask somebody to do X to make you feel good about yourself, but if you can do so, you may find that you massively improve your social life. For example, asking your friends to issue an invitation even if they know you will be busy may help, or encouraging your partner to give you positive feedback as well as criticism could make things easier.

Every person with ADHD will need different things from their relationships, but you should remember a few things: firstly, that women are often side-lined and overlooked as a result of their ADHD, and secondly, that they tend to undervalue their own needs and avoid asking for things because they do not want to be a nuisance.

Instead, focus on the fact that you are worthy enough to build good relationships, and encourage your friends to recognise your needs and meet them where they can.

You should also focus on slowing down and paying attention to what your friends need. People with ADHD often do struggle more to read other people and correctly assess their emotions, but that doesn't mean you shouldn't try. Make an effort to ask others how they are doing and to listen carefully to the responses, and think about ways in which you can make life a little easier and pleasanter for your friends.

This will help to build strong connections on both sides, and establish trusting bonds. Look for ways to both give and accept help, and you will find that your relationships get easier. We'll go into more detail in the following chapter.

How To Meet New People, Form New Friendships, and Pursue Romantic Relationships

If you are feeling isolated and alone, there is a high chance that you would love to expand your support network – but how do you do this? Meeting new people can be challenging when you aren't feeling good about yourself and your social skills, so how do you go about doing this?

You can often meet like-minded people by engaging in hobbies. For example, if you're an avid reader, join a book club or a group at your local library, and see if you connect with anybody there.

If you are a keen sportswoman, head for a gym or go running in the park. Whatever hobby brings you joy, look for ways to turn it into connections. This gives you a head-start because you will have an established shared interest to found your relationship on.

You should also tap into your existing network if applicable and use this to meet new people. Go to parties and events, or specifically ask your friends to introduce you to other people who they know. With an existing connection, you may find it easier to make friends, and this is a great way to expand your network.

Romantic relationships can be even harder, but for many people, the same techniques will work. Of course, you can also opt for dating apps, but you may find that romantic connections evolve organically out of the people you have met in other ways, and for many people, this is the easiest way to meet potential partners.

Once you've started to make connections, you need to make sure you follow up with them. It is really hard to make the time for this, so consider putting it on your upcoming schedule. Regular contact, even if it's only a quick chat or a few texts a week, is key to building relationships and showing your interest in the other person.

Most people are busy and struggle to make this kind of effort, so if you can do it, you'll set yourself apart from the crowd and massively increase your chances of making strong friendships.

It's also a good idea to make yourself a positive presence when you are first getting to know people, even if you are feeling low. If you are a black cloud at every party you attend, you'll put people off, possibly subconsciously. They will start to associate you with negativity, and this can have a bad effect on the relationship.

Be conscious of how you come across and try to be a source of positivity at least most of the time. This isn't to say that you should avoid ever complaining about anything, but remember that you want the overall impression to be positive. Being sour, uncommunicative, or full of complaints won't help you make friends.

Some people with ADHD find that it's hard to approach others in the first place, and if that rings true for you, consider setting yourself a mini goal. The next time you are out socialising, talk to at least 3 new people, and don't leave until you have done this. If that's too much of a challenge, try just 1 person, but make sure you are actually stretching your abilities and doing something that you find challenging.

Always go to social events with some sort of goal, and keep trying to expand your comfort zone and do something new.

How To Improve Your Current Relationships With Proven Tactics

In order to figure out how to make better relationships, you might find it helps to better understand what pitfalls make relationships hard for women with ADHD. I'm going to explore each in detail, along with tips for how to counteract that specific problem. Whether you want to pursue a romantic relationship or just a friendship, you should find that these cues help.

Forgetfulness

You are probably well aware of the sinking feeling that comes from realising you've missed a friend's birthday or another important event. This often causes hurt and frustration, especially if your presence was required somewhere.

You can mitigate it by finding a reminder system that works for you and always adding important dates to your calendar in advance. As soon as you make plans with somebody, write them down. You can also ask friends to follow up with you if it's appropriate for the situation.

Impulsiveness

If you aren't good at thinking before you act, you may find that this is detrimental to your relationships – especially with your partner. Things like shared finances can cause particular tension if you are an impulse buyer. It is important to be aware of your shortcomings here, and to try to find ways to mitigate them and reach compromises.

Setting up tricks to prevent yourself from spending money (e.g. carrying only cash, limiting how much you put in an account, not going to certain shops, etc.) may help to reduce friction.

You can apply this sort of impulsiveness restriction to your other relationships too – make a habit of checking whether something is okay with your friends before going ahead and doing it. This should decrease the chances of impulsiveness worsening your relationships.

Struggling To Listen

Many people with ADHD struggle to pay attention when other people are talking. You might find yourself checking your phone or interrupting them or gazing into space.

This can be hurtful to the other party. There are lots of techniques you can use to improve your "active listening" skills, so consider doing this. Things like making regular eye contact, asking questions, or repeating phrases that the other person has used may all help.

Repeating phrases might sound odd, but it's a really strong technique that will stop you from getting the wrong end of the stick. You might preface it with something like, "Let me check if I understand" or "I think you're saying…"

Doing this when you are unsure about the situation can increase the chances that it will go well. It gives the other person an opportunity to correct you if you have misunderstood something.

Social Miscues

If you find that you often struggle to read a situation and you cause friction because of it, don't be afraid to talk to your friends or romantic partner about this. There may be things that they can do to more clearly signal to you what they are thinking and feeling. Even if they can't make the communication perfectly smooth, you may be able to minimise misunderstandings.

They may also be more understanding when things go wrong if they recognise how hard you find certain cues.

You may find that you can improve your understanding of other people's body language by paying particular attention and verbally confirming how the person is feeling towards you.

These things should all help to minimise social difficulties and improve your ability to communicate – which will boost your relationships and make it easier to connect on both platonic and romantic levels.

Lack Of Organisation

Sometimes, your lack of organisation will also get in the way of your friendships or relationships. This can be physically, in how cluttered your home is, or emotionally.

If you are too disorganised to ever organise anything with your friends and you fail to uphold your commitments even with regular reminders, there is a chance that your friends will feel annoyed. They may feel like you don't want to make an effort to spend time with them, without understanding that being organised isn't about effort for people with ADHD.

You may find that having an honest conversation about the things you find challenging helps.

Discuss how hard you find it to put plans together. If you do have some organisation skills but you don't trust yourself to manage an entire event, consider whether you could help somebody else do it, so you're inputting something, even if you can't do everything.

Best Jobs For Women With ADHD

We talked earlier about playing to your strengths, and you can and should aim to do this in your career as well as your social life. Doing this will give you the best chances for success because it will ensure that you have a working environment that suits you. It will also make work pleasanter for you and for the people you work with.

There are a lot of jobs that will enhance your career and make your strengths shine, while minimising your weaknesses. You are far more likely to be promoted and feel good about yourself and the work you do if you choose a job that is suitable for someone with ADHD.

Fortunately, there are many options out there, so let's explore a few. Of course, you will need to think about other aspects of the job, like whether you have the skills/education/passion for it, but hopefully this list will help you.

Copy Editor

Do you enjoy working in a fast-paced environment? If so, copy editing could be for you. Turnaround times are often tight and the short deadlines may help you to stay on task and get a lot done.

You may also find that you are able to hyperfocus when you need to, giving you an edge over the challenges of the job.

Beautician

If you struggle with long-term projects and you always want to jump to the next thing, you might find that working as a beautician suits you. With this job, you will constantly have short-term goals and hands-on work to do. You will get to move from task to task, which many people with ADHD find more sustainable and engaging.

Software Developer

If you are always looking for something new to do, becoming a software developer might be the perfect career path. You will have the structure of designing software, but the demands of the job will constantly be changing. This can help you keep you challenged and engaged, and prevent the job from becoming monotonous.

Emergency Dispatcher

For those who need high stakes, high speed work, becoming an emergency dispatcher may be a great idea.

This is again an environment that will challenge you and make sure you are engaged, preventing any risk of boredom. Intense and urgent jobs tend to be the best for engaging people with ADHD, and this is a particularly focused work environment that will encourage you to hone your focus and stay on task at all times.

Fire Fighter

Like becoming an emergency dispatcher, you may find that the high stakes and urgency associated with this job help you to stay on task. Your ability to make snap decisions will become an advantage, and the adrenaline-rich and chaotic environment can often be a trigger for focused and powerful problem-solving. This is the sort of environment in which a person with ADHD can really thrive. Other emergency service jobs may be similarly helpful by challenging your mind and playing to your decision-making strengths.

Nurse

Being a nurse often means moving from task to task quickly, but staying very focused on a single person while you are dealing with them. This helps many people with ADHD to flourish.

You can deal directly with a patient and put all your energy and thought into them, and then move on to the next one before your attention gets jogged elsewhere.

Again, being a nurse may have the additional push of adrenaline, depending on the path you choose, so consider this as a secondary benefit of the job.

Preschool Teacher

You might be surprised at the idea of being a teacher, but many people with ADHD thrive in this sort of environment too. You will need to get your organisation skills up to scratch as much as possible, but this sort of work is often highly engaging, and it will constantly change and challenge you, keeping you engaged.

It will also utile your creative skills, and give you an opportunity to interact with others and help them learn and grow. The job can be immensely rewarding, and it's well worth considering this career path. If you don't want to work with young children, being a teacher for older kids may also be a great option, but it is worth being aware that this does frequently come with higher demands for being organised.

Certain Retail Jobs

You have to choose carefully when it comes to retail, but there are some retail jobs that are perfect for people with ADHD. Opt for somewhere busy, with a lot of foot traffic, and a constantly changing flow of duties, and you will probably find that you love it. Avoid slow shops and places where the duties never change, or you may find that you become bored and restless.

Musician

Creative jobs frequently appeal to those with ADHD, and a lot of women with this condition are highly creative. Music is a particularly common area of interest, and you might be able to find work as a professional musician, a DJ, or something similar. This could be a side job while you get established if necessary, or a full-time job if you are able to make it work.

Look at other creative industries too. Interior designers, engineering, art, dancing, fashion, architecture, and other jobs that call for creativity will often help people with ADHD to feel engaged in their work. These jobs also tend to keep changing, and they may have flexible hours and less rigid processes than some of the other industries.

The most important thing about choosing a job, however, is making sure you are passionate about it. That passion will carry you through when your ADHD is making things hard and you want to quit. If you love your job, you will be far more motivated to overcome the challenges that it presents. Choosing work that doesn't inspire you is a recipe for boredom, disengagement, lack of growth, and ultimately, failure.

It may sound trite to say do what you love, and this isn't always practical – but you should try to choose something that you have some emotional connection with and you are likely to find that your work is more fulfilling, more sustainable, and more enjoyable.

Improve Your Spending Habits In An Easy And Sustainable Way

If you have problems curbing your spending, you are probably looking for ways to get it under control – and doing so may help to make your life considerably less stressful. You can decrease or avoid going into debt, feel more comfortable with a safety net, and possibly improve your relationship with your partner if money is a contentious issue between you. So, how do you save money and stop spending as much money, and more importantly, how do you stick at it? Let's explore some top tricks.

Tip 1) Figure Out Your Income

The very first thing you need to do in order to start living within your means is to work out how much money you have coming in each month, and what your non-negotiable outgoings are. Tot up your income (making sure you account for tax if necessary) and remove your expenses, and this will give you an idea of what you can afford to spend each month. For example, if your income is £1500 per month, and you've accounted for food, groceries, rent (or mortgage), services, and any other essentials, you might find that you are left with £200 per month. This is the money that you have to play with.

Remember, you should always overestimate your expenses, setting aside a little extra money for emergencies or unexpected bills. Having a good grip on these numbers and understanding what your income is, what your expenses are, and what money you have available may make it easier to keep your spending on track.

Tip 2) Set Bigger Goals

Try thinking about the things that you want in life. What do you value? Would you love to save up for a big holiday or a course that will improve your employability, or are you passionate about doing up your home and making it beautiful?

Figuring out the things that really matter to you will make it much easier to determine what you should spend your money on, which may help you to avoid making frivolous purchases. Instead, you'll be encouraged to save up for the things that you truly want.

Tip 3) Avoid Carrying Money

Not having money on you when you are out and about – or carrying a limited budget – can be one of the most effective ways to curb spending. Some people find that working with cash or having a limited balance in their bank helps to minimise how much money they spend without meaning to. Leave excess funds behind, and you won't be able to go over the budget. Similarly, not keeping your credit card near your computer and not storing the payment information on there may help too. Make it harder for yourself to buy things online, and you will create a "pause" that gives your more rational brain time to kick in and decide whether you really want to buy the item or not.

Tip 4) Look At Your Spending Habits

Figuring out what you tend to spend money on can also help. Try saving up your receipts and once per month, sit and look at what you spent money on. Highlight areas that you are unhappy with, and look for ways to cut back in those areas.

Tip 5) Set Up Savings

You should also have a savings account that you transfer at least some money to each month. Count this as an actual expense when you do your budget, and set up an automatic transfer to make sure you save according to your plan, and you aren't tempted to spend that money instead.

Limit your access to this account by leaving the card at home and only dipping into the savings when you need to. These should be viewed as emergency savings.

You can apply this strategy in other ways, too. Some people decide to divide up their income so that they spend certain percentages on saving for certain things. For example, you might have a bank account where you specifically send funds intended for holiday savings, house or car repairs, taxes, etc.

Dividing your money up like this can help to ensure that the bulk of it is going to things that matter to you. You can also make a "spend freely" account so that you do get to indulge occasionally, but this indulgence is limited. This is often more effective than trying to stop spending completely.

Tip 6) Use Budgeting Apps

There are a lot of money management systems out there, so try some of them and see if they help you. Banking apps, finance trackers, and savings apps can all help you manage your money better. You might also find that building a spreadsheet that tracks your income and outgoings helps you to feel empowered and stay in control of your money on a long-term basis.

Fall Asleep Faster And Sleep Better On A Regular Basis

Sleep is one of the most important aspects of being productive and feeling healthy. A lot of women who suffer from ADHD find that their symptoms are much worse when they have slept badly – so how can you help yourself to fall asleep?

Tip 1) Adjust Gradually

If you are trying to adjust your sleep time, don't try to do it in huge leaps. You don't want to move your sleep by 5 hours in one day; this will leave you feeling disoriented and badly rested. Instead, move by about 20 minutes per day until you are on a schedule that feels more reasonable to you. For example, if you are currently falling asleep at 1 in the morning and you want to get to bed earlier, try switching off at 12:40. The following day, you can switch off at 12:20, and the next day, 12:00. Keep doing this until you reach your sleep goals, and then make efforts not to let it slip again.

Tip 2) Meditate Before Bed

A lot of people with ADHD find that they cannot make their mind switch off before bed. Sometimes, meditation will help.

Try some gentle yoga (but no strenuous exercise, as this will wake your brain up) or simply some deep breathing exercises.

This slowing down will send signals to your brain that it should be switching off and relaxing. This may help you to doze off when you lie down.

Tip 3) Use Darkness

You will sleep much better if you are able to make your room dark and comfortable. A sleep mask may help if you find you are often attempting to sleep when it's light out. Invest in blackout curtains or blinds, and avoid having a light left on in the room.

Before bed, you should make sure you are using dim lights, rather than bright ones, as these will help to trigger your brain's sleep response by simulating the sun going down.

Tip 4) Try Melatonin

It is thought that many people with sleep difficulties, especially those with ADHD, may not produce melatonin as they should.

Melatonin helps to regulate your circadian rhythm and ensures that you can fall asleep at the proper time

– but if your body isn't producing enough of it, you're very likely to find that you don't drop off easily.

You should discuss getting a melatonin supplement with your doctor.

Tip 5) Try A Weighted Blanket

Many people with ADHD find that weighted blankets are enormously beneficial, and help with anxiety, restlessness, difficulty falling asleep, and difficulty staying asleep. You will need to buy one that is right for your body weight, as this increases the chances that it will work well.

Tip 6) Practice Sleep Hygiene

There are a lot of rules associated with sleep hygiene, but here are a few of them:

- Keep your room clean and tidy, so that it is a relaxing space
- Avoid drinking caffeine for several hours before bed
- Don't eat a large meal just before you try to go to sleep
- Avoid exercising too close to bedtime
- Avoid working in your bedroom, or your brain may struggle to switch off from work when you lie down

- Make your bed comfortable and warm (but not hot) and regularly change your bedding so that you feel comfy in bed
- Do not use screens or other gadgets when you are in bed or during your wind-down period

You might find that taking a warm shower helps you to fall asleep, because your body will cool down afterwards, and this cooling process often triggers sleepiness.

Tip 7) Keep Your Room Cool

Being too hot at night will make it hard to fall asleep, and very hard to stay asleep. That means you should aim for your room to be cool (although not cold) when you are ready to go to bed.

Keep a window cracked or your door open, and don't use heavy blankets or thick pyjamas. You will sleep much better if you are cool enough.

Printed in Great Britain
by Amazon